LOOKING AFTER YOUR PET
Rabbit

Text by Clare Hibbert
Photography by Robert and Justine Pickett

A⁺

Titles in the LOOKING AFTER YOUR PET series:

• Cat • Dog • Hamster • Rabbit
• Guinea Pig • Fish

First published in 2003 by Hodder Wayland
338 Euston Road, London NW1 3BH
Hodder Wayland is an imprint of Hodder
Children's Books.
This edition published under license from
Hodder Wayland. All rights reserved.

Produced by White-Thomson Publishing Ltd.
2/3 St. Andrew's Place, Lewes, BN7 1UP
Copyright © 2004 White-Thomson Publishing

Editor: Elaine Fuoco-Lang, Interior Design:
Leishman Design, Cover design: Hodder
Wayland, Photographs: Robert Pickett,
Proofreader: Alison Cooper

Published in the United States by
Smart Apple Media
1980 Lookout Drive, North Mankato,
Minnesota 56003

Library of Congress Cataloging-in-Publication
Data

Hibbert, Clare, 1970–
Rabbit / text by Clare Hibbert ; photography by
Robert and Justine Pickett.
p. cm. — (Looking after your pet)
Summary: Introduces pet care for rabbits,
including such topics as feeding, grooming, and
visit to the veterinarian.
ISBN 1-58340-432-5
1. Rabbits—Juvenile literature. 2. Rabbits—
Health—Juvenile literature. [1. Rabbits. 2. Pets.]
I. Pickett, Robert, ill. II. Pickett, Justine, ill. III.
Title.

SF453.2.H53 2004
636.932'2—dc22   2003062393

9 8 7 6 5 4 3 2 1

Acknowledgments

The publishers would like to thank the following
for their assistance with this book:
The PDSA (Reg. Charity 283483) for their help
and assistance with the series.

With kind thanks for rabbits to Rosie Pilbrim an
the Animal Care Unit, Canterbury College, Kent.

The Web site addresses (URLs) included in this
book were valid at the time the book went to
press. However, because of the nature of the
Internet, it is possible that some addresses may
have changed, or sites may have changed or
closed down since publication.

Printed in China

Contents

Keeping a rabbit

The first question to ask yourself is, "Why do I want a rabbit?"

Rabbits are gentle and friendly. They make great pets. But before you decide a rabbit is the pet for you, make sure that you are ready to look after one. You will have to buy your rabbit a comfortable hutch and a run for the garden.

▶ Rabbits are soft to pet.
They make adorable, cuddly pets.

...bbits can live from 6

..2 years on average,

..d you will need to

..d and play with your

.. every day. You will

.. need to clean out

.. hutch and find

..neone to care for

..r pet when you go

.. vacation.

Pet Talk

How many rabbits?

..ou can keep one rabbit, but it might get lonely. If you keep
..ne rabbit, you must give it as much attention as possible.
.. is better to keep two. So long as you have your pets
..eutered (*see page 25*), it does not matter whether you
..eep two bucks (male rabbits), two does (female rabbits), or
..ne of each.

▲ If you have a pet guinea pig, you can let it graze in the run with your rabbit, but make sure you supervise the animals together. Provide each animal with its own hutch.

► This rabbit is a Lop.
See how its ears
hang down.

Choosing a rabbit

Look for a healthy baby rabbit.

▼ Don't be tempted to choose a rabbit you feel sorry for. Go for the liveliest of the litter.

Perhaps you know someone who has baby rabbits that nee good homes. If not, try a pet shop, breeder, or anin shelter. Baby rabbits are called "kittens." They can leave their mothers when the are around seven to nine weeks old

Choose the boldest kitten and as. to handle it. Then you can check its health. Ask how big your rabb will grow. Larger types might be t big for you to handle. Find out if your new pe is a buck a doe.

▲ When you take your new pet home, put it into its hutch right away. Leave it alone for a few hours to get used to its new surroundings.

nember to find out what
d your rabbit likes eating.
 for a little of its bedding to
 in its new hutch.

Top Tips

Choose a rabbit that has

❧ smooth, glossy fur with no bare patches

❧ bright, clear eyes and clean ears

❧ a clean, twitching nose—a sign that it is curious and playful

❧ neat teeth that fit together

❧ no overgrown claws

his rabbit looks healthy and alert. It will
nake a great pet if you look after it well.

Your rabbit's home

Prepare the hutch before you get your new pet.

For one medium-sized rabbit, the hutch should be at least 60 inches (150 cm) long, 24 inches (60 cm) wide, and 24 inches (60 cm) high. Buy a bigger hutch for two rabbits or one large rabbit.

The hutch should have a daytime area with a large wire-mesh door that lets in light and air. It will also need a connecting dark, cozy sleeping area with a solid wooden door. Be sure both doors close securely. The hutch should have a sloped, overhanging roof covered in heavy felt to help keep it waterproof. Put the hutch somewhere shaded from the sun and sheltered from the wind. The hutch should be raised off the ground to keep it dry.

▲ Building your rabbit a hutch can be fun, but make sure hutch is properly weatherproof. A sloping roof will allow rainwater to run off.

Top Tips

Weather beaters

- In heavy rain, cover the hutch with a tarp.

- In freezing weather, move the hutch into a shed. Do not move it into a garage used by cars, though. Exhaust fumes can kill rabbits.

- Do not put the hutch in a greenhouse—it will be too hot.

Put your rabbit's hutch in a sheltered spot, out of direct sunlight.

All rabbits will need a cozy home to live in. If you buy a hutch, make sure it is the right size for your rabbit.

Inside the hutch

Make the hutch into a cozy home.

Line the hutch with newspaper and wood shavings. Do not use sawdust, which can damage your pet's breathing. Fill the sleeping area with hay. Attach a water bottle to the mesh door. You should also attach a hay rack to hold clean hay for your rabbit to eat. Put the food dishes in the daytime area. Add a piece of wood for your rabbit to gnaw—this will stop its teeth from growing too long.

▼ Get your rabbit's hutch ready before bring your new pet home. Use the checklist to make sure you haven't forgotten anything.

Checklist: hutch kit

Plastic drip-feed water bottle

Two pottery food bowls—one for dried and one for fresh food

Hay bedding

Newspaper

• Wood shavings

• Fruit-tree branch or gnawing block

• Litter tray (*see page 21*)

▼ Use hay, not straw, for your rabbit's sleeping area. Straw stalks might hurt your pet's eyes.

Feeding your rabbi

Your rabbit needs regular meals.

Wild rabbits eat seeds, roots, and grasses. You
can feed your pet special rabbit food, which is
a mix of dried cereal, seeds, and rabbit pellets.
Eating dry food is thirsty work, so keep your
pet's water bottle full. You should also give
fresh fruit and vegetables to your rabbit
(*see page 14*).

▼ The water bottle should always ha
clean water for your pet to drink. F
it with fresh water every day.

d your rabbit every morning. In addition to the

d mix, give your rabbit hay in a special hay rack.

ach the rack on the inside of the door so the

does not get wet when it rains.

▶ Make sure there is always fresh, sweet hay for your rabbit. Hay is very good for its teeth.

Top Tips

Feeding kit

❧ Put your rabbit's food in a heavy pottery dish that it cannot knock over.

❧ Do not put a plastic food bowl in the hutch. Your rabbit will gnaw it, and the sharp edges might hurt the rabbit's mouth.

❧ Use a drip-feed water bottle rather than a water bowl, which might spill.

▼ If you feed your pet mixed rabbit food, always provide hay, too. Some vets believe it is better for rabbits to eat only grass and hay.

Fresh foods

Your rabbit loves its greens!

Treat your rabbit to some fresh food every evening.
About a handful is enough—too much will give
your rabbit a tummy ache. Always wash fresh
food first.

Give your rabbit raw root vegetables, such as
carrots, parsnips, and turnips. Once it is older
than 12 weeks, you can also feed it greens
including spinach and sprouts. Try peas,
cauliflower, celery, and parsley,
too, but not lettuce—it can give
your rabbit an upset tummy.

▶ Many fruits and vegetables are
good for your pet—but only in
small amounts. Take care not to
give too many fresh treats.

a treat, give your rabbit a slice of apple or pear,
even a strawberry. You will soon learn what
r rabbit likes best.

ver leave uneaten fresh food in the hutch for
re than a day, or it will go bad.

This rabbit is enjoying a nibble
of parsley. Use the checklist to
make sure you do not feed your
rabbit any poisonous plants.

Checklist: wild plants

heck wild foods with an adult. Your rabbit can eat:

- Chickweed
- Clover
- Dandelions

- Groundsel
- Shepherd's purse
- Yarrow

ut these plants are poisonous:

- Bindweed
- Buttercups
- Deadly nightshade
- Flowering bulbs
- Foxgloves

- Lily of the valley
- Poppies
- Privet

Together time

Handle your rabbit every day to keep it tame and friendly.

For the first couple of days, just talk to your pet so that it gets used to your voice.

Then you can begin to stroke and handle your rabbit. Scoop both hands under your pet's body and lift. Hold the rabbit close to your chest so that it feels safe and does not wriggle.

▶ As long as it feels safe, your rabbit will enjoy being cuddled and petted.

If your rabbit is long-haired, you will need to brush its coat every day. Short-haired rabbits like being groomed, too. Use an old, soft hairbrush—one that is only used for brushing your rabbit. Never try to bathe your rabbit.

◀ Brush your rabbit with light, firm strokes. Always brush away from the head, towards the tail.

▼ The more you handle your rabbit, the tamer it will become. Find out where it likes to be tickled—but be gentle.

Top Tips

Rabbit handling

- Do not disturb your rabbit if it is sleeping.
- Never try to pick up your rabbit only by the scruff of its neck or by the ears.
- Be gentle! Never shout at or hit your rabbit.
- Always put your rabbit back into its hutch bottom-first so it cannot kick you.

Playing outside

Like you, your rabbit needs exercise.

In the wild, rabbits are free to run around. Your pet needs to stretch its legs, too. Your rabbit will enjoy being in a "run." Most runs are triangular-shaped and made of wire mesh. There should be a shaded section at one end where your rabbit can rest. Move the run around the lawn to give your rabbit fresh grass to nibble. Remember to attach your rabbit's water bottle to the side of the run.

▼ Your rabbit can graz
fresh grass if you bu
ark like this one.

fine days, you can put your rabbit

 run called a "grazing ark." But

r put the ark on grass that has

 treated with weedkiller.

▼ This lucky pet has its own rabbit playground! If you have the space, ask an adult to help you build one. Your pet will have space to run around in safety.

Pet Talk

Rabbit playground

 you have space, make a rabbit playground. Put a six-foot (1.8 m) high
ence around your rabbit's hutch. This must be sunk about 12 inches
(30 cm) into the ground so that your rabbit cannot burrow out. Cover the
op with mesh to keep out cats, and place a ramp up to the hutch.

▶ Being outside on a sunny day is very good for your pet—so long as it has somewhere shady to rest. Sunshine helps the rabbit to stay healthy.

Rabbit habits

Your rabbit rubs its head against you to be friendly.

Some rabbits lick their owners, too! If your rabbit kicks or bites, say "No" in a firm voice, then put it back in its hutch. It will soon learn not to be naughty.

You may train your rabbit outdoors. You can also let your rabbit explore in the house. Make sure there are no electric cords around for it to chew. Some people keep their pet rabbit in the house all the time. House rabbits need a lot of attention and training.

► You can train your rabbit to come when you hold out some food. Do this in the yard, but first make sure there is no way your rabbit can escape.

Pet Talk

Toilet training

House rabbits can be toilet trained. Outside rabbits can learn to use a mini litter tray, too—and it helps with cleaning up. Use a jar lid filled with wood shavings. Add some soiled shavings to show your pet what the litter tray is for.

House rabbits must be trained to use a litter tray. Never use a plastic one that your pet could chew. A tin or enamel roasting pan would be ideal.

▽ Your pet can play indoors. Keep any doors shut and do not let your rabbit climb stairs. Keep it away from houseplants, too.

Cleaning up

Do not let your pet's hutch get dirty.

Check the hutch every day and take out any leftover food. Remove your rabbit's droppings and any wet bedding. Wash the food bowls and water bottle in warm, soapy water and rinse well. Clean the hutch thoroughly once a week. Put your rabbit somewhere safe, such as its exercise run. Clear away all the old bedding, wood shavings, and newspaper. Brush or scrape dirt from the floor.

▶ Use a bottle brush to thoroughly clean the water bottle. Rinse well before you refill it with clean water.

w put down fresh
wspaper and wood
avings. Fill the
sting area with
an hay. Every
nth or so, scrub the
tch with a special
disinfectant. Rinse
ay all trace of
infectant. Wait for
hutch to dry out
npletely before you
in the clean
dding.

▲ It is a good idea to wear rubber gloves when cleaning out your rabbit's hutch. A scrubbing brush should get rid of any caked-on dirt.

Checklist: cleaning kit

eep all your cleaning equipment together. Use
ese only for cleaning out your rabbit hutch.

Rubber gloves

Soap

Bottle brush

Sponge

Dustpan and brush

Scraper

Scrubbing brush

Plastic bowl or bucket for
hot water

Special pet disinfectant

Rags or paper towels

Rabbit health

Even healthy rabbits need to visit the vet once a year.

The vet will check your pet's health and give shots to prevent serious diseases, such as myxomatosis. He or she will help treat fleas and also clip your rabbit's claws or teeth if they are too long. Never try to do this yourself.

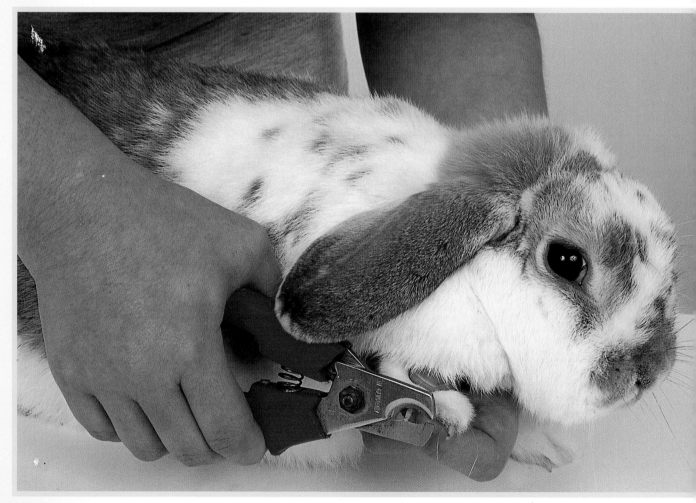

▲ Rabbits' claws never stop growing. If they become too long, take your pet to the vet to have its claws clipped.

aby rabbits are cute, but it is not a good idea
) let your pet have babies. Ask
our vet about neutering.

You will also need to visit your vet to have your pet neutered. Talk to your vet about this when your rabbit has its first check-up. Neutering stops female rabbits from having babies and can cut down on bad behavior in male rabbits, such as fighting. It is best not to breed rabbits—there are already too many unwanted pets that need homes.

Checklist: illness

you see any of these signs of illness,
ake your rabbit to the vet:

Dull fur

Sores on its skin

Dirty ears

Runny eyes

Sneezing

No appetite

Diarrhea (upset tummy)

Worms in its droppings

Bloated tummy

Not being very active
or alert

▼ You should check your pet's skin and fur each day while you are handling it. The fur should gleam and the skin should be smooth.

Vacation time

When you go on vacation, do not forget your pet.

Ask someone to come and feed your pet twice a day and fill up the hay and water. It might be easier to take the hutch, food, and equipment to a friend's house.

Write a list of what to do. Add your vet's telephone number in case your rabbit is sick. Spend time showing your friend how to handle your pet. Then your rabbit will not be frightened when you are away.

If you cannot find anyone to care for your rabbit, ask your vet for advice.

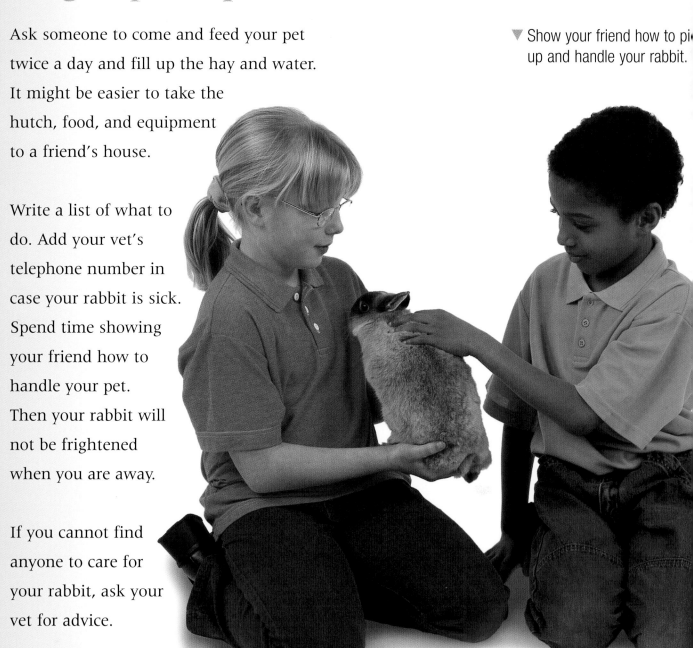

▼ Show your friend how to pi
up and handle your rabbit.

26

Pet Talk

Meeting other animals

If your friend has rabbits, it is probably better to keep them apart from yours. Rabbits do not get along with cats or dogs either. If your friend has one of these, make sure he or she will be able to keep them away from your pet.

▲ Your pet might fight with your friend's rabbit. Make sure they are kept apart, even when they are grazing in the yard.

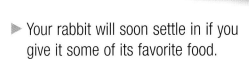

► Your rabbit will soon settle in if you give it some of its favorite food.

Rabbit facts

Bet you didn't know that rabbits have lived in North America for 40 million years! Read on for more fantastic facts.

- Rabbits' teeth never stop growing.

- The two most common wild rabbits are European rabbits and American cottontails. All pet rabbits are tame types from Europe.

- Wild rabbits live underground in "warrens."

- Hares are related to rabbits, but they have longer ears and legs.

- A group of rabbits is called a "herd."

- There are more than 50 different breeds of pet rabbit. The most popular is the Dutch.

Rex rabbits are special breeds that have
t and velvety coats.

Hair from Angora rabbits is spun into
ol. In one year, you could collect about
pounds (500 g) from one rabbit—enough
a very soft, fluffy sweater!

The rabbit breed with the longest ears is
English Lop. One male, measured in 1996,
ears that were 30 inches (75 cm) long!

Two New Zealand rabbits
re the record for the largest
er. Both had 24 kittens.

The largest rabbit breed is
White Flemish Giant. It
weigh up to 17.7 pounds
<g)—about the same as a toddler!

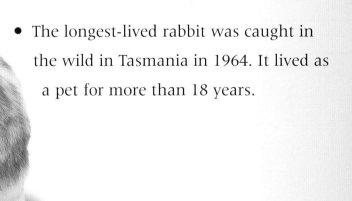

- The longest-lived rabbit was caught in
  the wild in Tasmania in 1964. It lived as
  a pet for more than 18 years.

Glossary

Animal shelter
A place that looks after lost or abandoned animals.

Breed
A particular type of rabbit, such as a Dutch, a Dwarf, or an English Lop.

Breeder
Someone who keeps rabbits to mate them and produce babies to sell. He or she will want to produce kittens of a particular breed or type.

Buck
A male rabbit.

Disinfectant
A cleaning fluid that kills germs. Ask your vet or pet shop for a mild disinfectant that is suitable for cleaning your rabbit's hutch. Follow the instructions with care.

Doe
A female rabbit.

Fleas
Insect pests that sometimes live on rabbits. Ask your vet for advice on how to get rid of fleas.

Grazing ark
A triangular run, made of wire mesh, that you can put your rabbit in while it grazes on your lawn. The ark should have a shaded area at one end.

Grooming
Cleaning a rabbit's fur. Short-haired rabbits can groom themselves, but long-haired ones need you to help by brushing them so they don't get hair balls. (Pellets of hair that can clog up a rabbit's throat).

Kitten
A baby rabbit.

Litter tray
A shallow container where an animal can go to the bathroom. If you have a house rabbit, you can train it to use a large litter tray. A roasting pan of enamel or tin is ideal. Never give your rabbit a plastic litter tray.

Myxomatosis
A disease that kills rabbits and is extremely contagious.

Neutering
Removing a rabbit's sex organs. This stops females from getting pregnant and makes males less likely to get into fights with other rabbits.

Shots
Injections that protect against serious disease.

Vet
Short for veterinarian. An animal doctor.

Further Information

Books

Alderton, David. *Rabbit: Looking After My Pet.* New York: Lorenz Books, 2002.

Baglio, Ben M. and Shelagh McNicholas. *Bunnies in the Bathroom.* Pittsburgh: Apple, 2000.

Foran, Jill. *Caring for Your Rabbit.* Calgary: Weigl, 2003.

Holub, Joan. *Why Do Rabbits Hop? And Other Questions About Rabbits, Guinea Pigs, Hamsters, and Gerbils.* New York: Dial, 2003.

Loves, June. *Guinea Pigs and Rabbits.* Broomall, Penn.: Chelsea House, 2003.

Tripp, Penny. *Animal Rights.* Mankato, Minn.: Thameside Press, 2003.

Trunbauer, Lisa. *The Life Cycle of a Rabbit.* Mankato, Minn.: Pebble Books, 2003.

Useful addresses

American Rabbit Breeders Association
www.arba.net

The American Society for the Prevention of Cruelty to Animals (ASPCA)
www.aspca.org

Humane Society of Canada
www.humanesociety.com

Humane Society of the United States
www.hsus.org

Index